Be Your Own

Boss

BE A BOSS, NOT JUST A LEADER

Time to Thrive

Siam Pasarly and Robert Farrell

Be Your Own Boss
Copyright © Siam Pasarly 10/28/2022

All Rights Reserved

No part of this book may be reproduced in any form,
by photocopying or by any electronic or mechanical means,
including information storage or retrieval systems,
without permission in writing from the copyright.

Be a Boss, Not Just a Leader
Siam Pasarly and Robert Farrell

www.siampasarly.com
www.youtube.com/siampasarly
+1 773 410 0092

Dedicated to my wife, Spozhmai Pasarly, with whom I started my own business, solved problems, and earned respect and money (even though we lost all our money within twenty-four hours).

To my daughter Malala Pasarly, my love, my life, and my light – I miss you so much.

To my son, Qiamuden, to whom I couldn't give more love.

Siam Pasarly

To Wren, Bella, and Jessica

And to my Muse

Robert Farrell

Table of Contents

Contents

1. Introduction 8
2. Definitions 14
   a. Boss 15
   b. Entrepreneur 17
   c. Businessperson 20
   d. Investor 21
3. Why Be Your Own Boss? 22
4. The Advantages of Being Your Own Boss 26
   a. You Work for Your Own Dreams 28
   b. Freedom! 30
   c. You're the Owner of Your Time 32
   d. You Can Have Financial Stability 33
   e. The Government Appreciates You 35
   f. You Can Become a Business Celebrity 36
   g. You Enhance Your Business Network 38
   h. You Set Your Own Work Style 39
   i. You Will Have Greater Expectations and More Confidence 40
   j. You Can Be Creative 41

5. Why the World Needs Bosses More Than Leaders .42
   a. The Boss Gets the Job Done....................43
   b. The Boss Says "I" before "We"...................44
   c. The Boss Focuses on Details or "Micro-Management"................45
   d. The Boss Values Productivity *and* People....47
   e. The Boss Takes Command............................50
   f. The Boss Inspires by Being Clear 52
   g. Leaders Say, "Let's Go!" but the Boss Says, "Go!"................53
   h. The Boss Knows Profits Can Change the World................54
   i. The Boss Has the Right Mindset....................56
   j. The Boss Has a Clear Vision 57
   k. The Boss Is Self-Disciplined 58
   l. The Boss Expects People to Succeed............59
   m. The Boss Has Strong People Skills 61
6. The Boss Avoids These Mistakes 62
   a. The Boss Isn't Disrespectful of Other Opinions 63
   c. Bosses Do Not Lose Control of Their Emotions 66
   d. The Boss Doesn't Bother Employees on Vacation................68
   e. The Boss Doesn't Tell Employees, "You Are Lucky to Have a Job."................70

....70

    f.   **The Boss Isn't Mistrustful**................................71

    g.   **The Boss Doesn't Criticize Publicly and Praise Privately** 73

7.   Thirteen Things a Boss Should Never Forget..........74

    a.   **The Boss Pays Attention to Profit and Loss**.75

    b.   **The Boss Values Time** 76

    c.   **The Boss Is Straightforward**..........................77

    d.   **The Boss Knows When to Say "No."**............78

    e.   **The Boss Keeps Notes and Records**...........80

    f.   **The Boss Follows the Protocol** 82

    g.   **The Boss Has Action Plans** 84

    h.   **The Boss Builds an Outstanding Team**........86

    i.   **The Boss is Results- or Outcomes-Oriented** 87

8.   What Kills Your Career as a Boss 89

    a.   **Not Making Your Business a Full-Time Commitment.**..90

    b.   **Not Having a Written Schedule** 91

    d.   **Not Having a Reason Why** 93

    e.   **Not Talking to the Most Important People.** ...94

    f.   **Not Having Guidance.** 95

    g.   **Not Taking Care of Yourself.** 96

9.   How to Behave like a Boss until You Are a Boss 97

    a.   **Take Complete Responsibility for Your Job.** 99

- b. Learn Every Aspect of Your Job. 100
- c. Take on Extra Responsibilities. 101
- d. Practice Your People Skills. 102
- e. Work Longer Hours. 103
- f. Develop Yourself. 104
10. Conclusion 105
11. References 108

Be Your Own Boss and Drive Your Life

1. Introduction

If you dare to walk and work with great bosses, you too can become a great Boss.

Being a great boss doesn't require a lot of money, but it does require courage, a powerful idea, making the right decisions, and action!

Usually, millionaires and successful businesspeople are too busy with their business operations. They don't have time to share their advice or write about their experiences. I had the same problem. I was so busy it was hard to take all my phone calls. I had a tight schedule; I had to focus on my business.

Suddenly, everything changed.

The Taliban captured all of Afghanistan, and I had no option but to leave the country in a hurry and become a refugee in the United States. I was in a refugee camp for six months. While others played, relaxed, or wasted their time, I realized I had a golden opportunity: I wrote three books.

Be Your Own Boss is the first book.

In Be Your Own Boss, I want to share my experience and the value of being your own Boss. Being your own Boss is not easy. The tough role is given to the strong player.
Even though I had to leave everything behind - my business, my money, and, worst of all, my family and friends - I didn't quit. I bounced back as a one-person army and established my new business in the United States of America.

I focus on being your own Boss because I have worked with multinational and multicultural companies, NGOs, and government entities for over fifteen years. Then I started my own business and learned that working for others is great when you are new in the market or don't have experience, but not always. Starting your own business is a reward. I worked with easy and challenging bosses, and, to be honest, I learned more from my tough Boss. After many years of experience working for others and running my own business, I recommend being your own Boss.

I emphasize "Be Your Own Boss" because the current world and enterprise market needs qualified, innovative, creative, and straightforward bosses who will initiate and lead the industries.

I want you to be your own Boss to implement your dreams and vision.

Thus don't be shy to use the word Boss. This word gives energy, motivation, power, and solid control. The upcoming chapters explain the details of being your Boss.

It is important to mention that the word "Boss" has been misperceived and constantly compared with a leader unfairly. We have great bosses who founded and led multinational companies, such as Mark

Zuckerberg, Elon Musk, Jack Ma, and others. We urge you to own the title "Boss" with pride.

You're responsible and in charge, so be proud to be in charge. Don't be apologetic or tiptoe around the word "Boss." Most people use other titles, such as foreman, supervisor, director, Chief Executive officer, Team Leader, Coach, President, Vice President, Chairperson, and many others. To be clear, to the people who report to you or to whom you assign a specific task, you're the Boss.

Publishing this book would not have been possible without Robert Farrell's co-authorship and Linda Keane's editing, my family and friends' emotional support, networking, and encouragement of Soraya Tonos, Bob Tonos, and Asmaa Rashid.

To determine if it's time to be your own Boss, read this book, perhaps many times, and ask why you are thinking of taking the leap.

Be Your Own Boss.

Siam Pasarly

Note: Being your own Boss is not just about becoming wealthy. Wealth is only one of the goals. Equally important are your health, your family, and your relationships. I knew financially successful people, but they valued money above all else. As a result, they damaged their health and relationships and even lost their lives. Being your own Boss means driving your own life, while at the same time valuing that which is even more important than money.

2. Definitions

a. <u>Boss</u>

The word "Boss" is derived from the Dutch word "baas," originally a term of respect used to address a person in charge of or responsible for the business. This term is still used in fifty-seven languages. For example, Indonesians say "bos," and Koreans say "boseu."

Despite its worldwide use, the word "Boss" is often misunderstood. It is often and inaccurately compared with the word "leader." Some great bosses founded and led multinational companies, such as Mark Zuckerberg, Elon Musk, Jack Ma, and others. So own the title "Boss" with pride. You're responsible and in charge. Be in charge. Don't be apologetic or tiptoe around the word Boss.

Most people use other titles, such as foreman, supervisor, director, Chief Executive Officer, Team Leader, Coach, President, Vice President, Chairperson, and many others. But to the people who report to you or to whom you assign specific tasks, whatever your title is, you're The Boss.

In this book, the word "Boss" is someone who manages and controls the organization he created and the staff he hired to achieve a specific goal or set of goals. This definition is easy to understand and is also the scope and purpose of this book.

Like a Boss

b. Entrepreneur

The Boss is also an entrepreneur. An entrepreneur establishes, organizes, and operates a business, taking on risks, usually financial, to do so. The entrepreneur creates and grows a business through creative ideas. According to the Indeed Editorial Team, "Entrepreneurs play key roles besides generating income as they grow their businesses." [1]

So profit isn't the only goal. The entrepreneur is trying to creatively solve a problem or develop a new product or service for the market.[2]

---

[1] The Indeed Editorial Team is a group of writers and researchers who cover insights and trends in the modern worlds of work, recruiting and HR.

[2] Tabitha Njogu graduated from Jomo Kenyatta University of Agriculture and Technology with a Bachelor's Degree in Commerce. She then specialized in Finance and Business Administration. Read more: Difference Between Entrepreneur and Businessman | Difference Between

The term "entrepreneur" comes from the French meaning "to undertake." In French, the verb "entreprendre" means "to undertake," with "entre" coming from the Latin word meaning "between" and "prendre," meaning "to take." "Entrepreneur" also sounds close to the Sanskrit word "anthaprerna," which means self-motivation."[3]

---

http://www.differencebetween.net/business/difference-between-entrepreneur-and-businessman/#ixzz7a0UjdQLR
[3] Etymology of the word "entrepreneur, entrepreneurship, Series on Entrepreneurial Culture

Leader

Leader is someone who influences and inspires others in order to accomplish goals. The leader holds a dominant position and leads by example. He has a vision and stays committed to a purpose. The leader sets a standard, so people become motivated and follow in her footsteps. According to Surbhi S, "A leader is someone who leads his followers, inspires, motivates, and guides them in different matters."

Later, we will discuss the crucial difference between a boss and a leader.

c. **Businessperson**

Business person is someone who sets up a private entity or business, most of the time with an existing idea to generate more money by offering products and services to the customers. Or a businessperson is an individual who has ownership or holding share over a company and undertakes activities to generate cash flow, revenue, and sales by using a combination of financial, human, intellectual, and physical capital to fuel economic development and growth.

d. <u>Investor</u>

An investor is a person or organization that invests in someone else's business idea by providing money or resources and may share in the financial success of the person or organization in which they have invested.

3. Why Be Your Own Boss?

Be your Own Boss

Today it is easier than ever to make a living doing what you love. The world is also more connected than ever. As a result, there are more opportunities and a need for bosses and entrepreneurs. However, if you are stuck in a job or working under someone else's supervision, you may find the world can be monotonous. I have worked with many multinational organizations in significant positions. They were excellent experiences, but I was never as happy or as financially successful as I have been in my own business. Being my own Boss meant I could implement my own ideas, work as late as I wanted, wake up when I wanted, throw parties with partners, and enjoy many other freedoms.

Being self-employed is hard work, but it is worth every sleep-deprived moment.

Be a Boss, Not Just a Leader

You're not alone if you think you would love to be your own Boss. Millions of others are thinking the same thing. According to a recent report by FreshBooks, 27 million Americans were expected

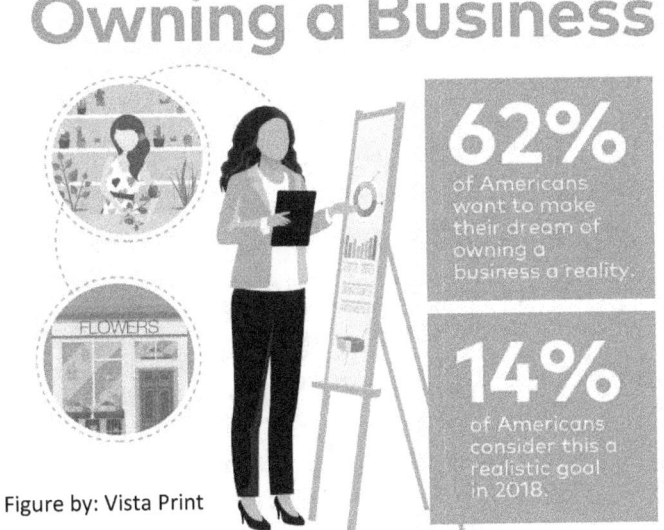

Figure by: Vista Print

to leave their jobs to be their own Boss by 2020. This number is increasing fast, with more than 10 million by 2022.[4] According to a Vistaprint report, three in five, or 62% of Americans ages 18 to 25, want to start their own business. To determine whether it's time to be your own Boss, read this

---

[4] https://www.oberlo.com/statistics/how-many-americans-are-self-employed

book, perhaps many times, and ask yourself why you are thinking of taking the leap.

4. The Advantages of Being Your Own Boss

Being your own Boss can be a liberating and thrilling experience. If you are self-motivated and comfortable with taking and managing risks, then starting your own business is an excellent way to express your creativity, manage your own time, and, of course, make money. It is not easy to be your own Boss; you will work longer hours, day and night, and on weekends, longer than you would at a conventional job. You might also experience steep monetary losses, but if you are persistent, patient, and resourceful, you can improve your odds of building a great business personalized to your needs.

Below are some crucial advantages to being your own Boss.

a. **<u>You Work for Your Own Dreams</u>**

Being your own Boss means working for your own dreams, not someone else's. You have the power to create a business that is consistent with your values, objectives, and goals and then infuse every aspect of its operations with your vision. Even if you don't have enough income initially, because you are working for your vision, it will help move you past discouraging times. And in working for your vision, you will attract opportunities in the form of partners and investors.

Bosses believe, "If you don't build your dream, someone else will hire you to help make theirs." Tony Gaskins"[5]

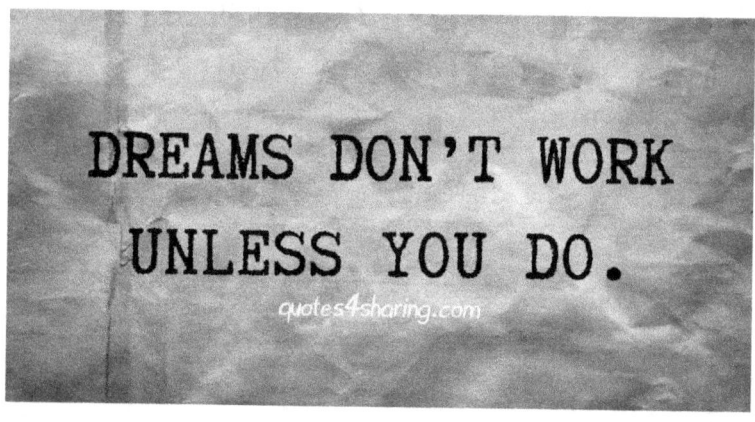

---

[5] Tony Gaskins is a motivational speaker, author and life coach. Having appeared on The Oprah Winfrey Show, The Tyra Banks Show and TBN's 700 Club.

b. **Freedom!**

Very few things are more important than freedom. Freedom is foundational. The more freedom an individual, group, or country has, the more it can move forward and progress. Placing ourselves under someone else's authority limits our freedom. Sometimes it is necessary. But working for ourselves, for our own dreams and goals, empowers us to truly make a difference in the world.

I remember the tension and obstacles I faced when working for others. In my country, Afghanistan, job security is a big problem. Often one would wake up, check his email and see his termination letter. Although I worked in significant positions with national and international organizations for over seven years, built my network, earned enough, traveled to many countries, and attended many conferences, I didn't have peace of mind until I started my own company. Then I began to feel free, proud, powerful, and self-reliant. Nothing was more enjoyable.

> **I didn't have peace of mind until I started my own company.**

c. <u>**You're the Owner of Your Time**</u>

Time management goes hand-in-hand with freedom.

You don't need a routine schedule when you start your own business. You have the freedom to decide what works best for you. Sometimes when you're in the mood to work, you work a lot. When required to work late, you may sleep until 11:00 a.m. the next day without worrying if someone will get angry or ask why you were late. As your own Boss, you create your own schedule. Although many business owners work longer hours than expected, they still have the flexibility to reorganize their tasks to start later in the day, take vacations and prioritize personal emergencies.

"There is no hand to catch time."

d. <u>You Can Have Financial Stability</u>

Being your own Boss not only helps solve societal problems, but it also feeds you. Although business owners are vulnerable to financial losses, they are also capable of earning virtually unlimited income. I've never heard of someone who became rich quickly through a traditional job. Entrepreneurs and business owners can earn substantial profits once they set up their companies efficiently and effectively.

It is essential to know you may not achieve financial independence immediately. Many entrepreneurs give up in five years or less. But for many who persevere, financial independence comes and, with it, the ability to truly enjoy life and take care of those you love.

"Most billionaires have one thing in common: None of them are employed."

Desiree Peralta [6]

---

[6] Desiree Peralta, Editor of The Brave Writer and With love, Dessy·writing on Finance, Investing, Life Lessons, Life, and Entrepreneurship.

e. <u>The Government Appreciates You</u>

When you start your own business, you hire people, which reduces unemployment. In addition, you pay taxes and make investments, which benefits the government. Governments around the world try to attract national and international investments. They even provide investment incentives, conducting investment events and summits to generate more revenue. The government values you and your investment.

In the beginning, in some countries, it may seem like the government doesn't appreciate you at all. You may find yourself paying prohibitive taxes that are not commensurate with the small number of earnings you have in the beginning. This is why it is essential to plan for this, to know what you want, and to persevere.

f. <u>You Can Become a Business Celebrity</u>

You may have heard of Elon Musk, Jack Ma, Mark Zuckerberg, Bill Gates, Alokozai, Steve Jobs, Jeff Bezos, Mukesh Ambani, Shahid Khan, Oprah, Hussain Sajwani, and many other international business celebrities. In the beginning, they were not well-known. But they succeeded, and their names are now recognized as market leaders in the national and international business communities.

Billionaire wealth is accumulating at an amazing speed. Below is a snapshot of the world's richest in 2022, based on data from the Forbes Real-Time Billionaires List in March 2022.

Be your Own Boss

Figure by: www.visualcapitalist.com 8

g. <u>You Enhance Your Business Network</u>

When you start your own company, you will have meetings with CEOs, business owners, government officials, media, customers, partners, business communities, and many other people and organizations. You will attend exhibitions and conferences to promote your business and ideas. You will surround yourself with the people you want. Great bosses know how to create and maintain relationships for win-win situations.

"If you want to go fast, go alone. If you want to go far, go together."

African Proverb

h. <u>You Set Your Own Work Style</u>

People have different work styles. Some love to work at home, listen to music and drink tea. Others prefer state-of-the-art facilities. And others need a calm place to work. When you start your own business, you're the Boss, so create a workplace that works for you.

The freedom to determine how you will use your time is invaluable. It is part of the freedom of being your own Boss.

"The key is in not spending time, but in investing it."
Stephen R. Covey

i. <u>You Will Have Greater Expectations and More Confidence</u>

Although they often started small, many bosses often became market leaders because of New entrepreneurs tend to be more confident and have higher morale due to their financial independence and business growth.

A big part of your increased confidence comes from deciding every day to be your own Boss and doing what it takes to succeed.

j. <u>You Can Be Creative</u>

It is essential to have freedom of thought, creativity, and the freedom to innovate. As your own Boss, you can direct your powers the way you prefer in your day-to-day operations. Even if you're not in a creative arena, being your own Boss allows you to flex your creative muscles daily.

From marketing, branding, public relations, problem-solving, and technology – all these tasks enable you to innovate and think outside the box.

When you're the Boss, you can't reinvent the wheel, but you can certainly improve upon it.

5. Why the World Needs Bosses More Than Leaders

a. **The Boss Gets the Job Done**

Leadership has been romanticized over the last forty years. The intention was good. Much of the literature describes how leaders are at the forefront, making bold choices, inspiring others, and keeping the company moving. Meanwhile, bosses are portrayed as middle management who do nothing but follow orders blindly and make life hard for their employees. There are indeed many bosses like this. But there are just as many, if not more, who focus on creating a powerful and effective company and getting the job done. They can also inspire, but more importantly, effective bosses create a focus for themselves and their employees. This is the kind of Boss you can be.

"While others were dreaming about it, I was getting it done."

Nathan W. Morris

b. The Boss Says "I" before "We"

People believe bosses are not as inclusive as leaders. They also believe bosses use the word "I" more than the word "we." But "I" might be the best word because the Boss takes the credit or blame for the actions and results of the organization. People who don't believe in their own capabilities or results use the word "we" to share the blame or put it on others. Results can't be hidden in the digital world.

The Boss is in charge of and responsible for everything.

If she hires a great team, achieves the goal, controls the staff, expects accountability, and manages the organization, she deserves to get the credit as well. When the organization is successful, the Boss says, "we." But the Boss should never forget to give credit to anyone who has helped the organization reach its goals. Taking too much credit will undermine the team and, ultimately, the organization.

Be your Own Boss

c. **The Boss Focuses on Details or "Micro-Management"**

Some bosses have been blamed for being overly focused on details or being micromanagers. Yet, recent studies by authors such as Gary Bradt,[7] emphasize the idea that small things make significant differences. Robert Collier[8] states, "Success is the sum of small efforts repeated daily." Hundreds of authors and motivational speakers believe in the power of small things to cause outstanding results. Lax bosses who don't focus on the small details will die before they are born to the market.

---

[7] Dr. Gary Bradt is a keynote speaker, leadership consultant and the author of *The Ring in the Rubble: Dig Through Change and Find Your Next Golden Opportunity* (McGraw-Hill, 2007). Go to www.GaryBradt.com for more information.

[8] Collier is an American author best known for his self-help and New Thought metaphysical books.

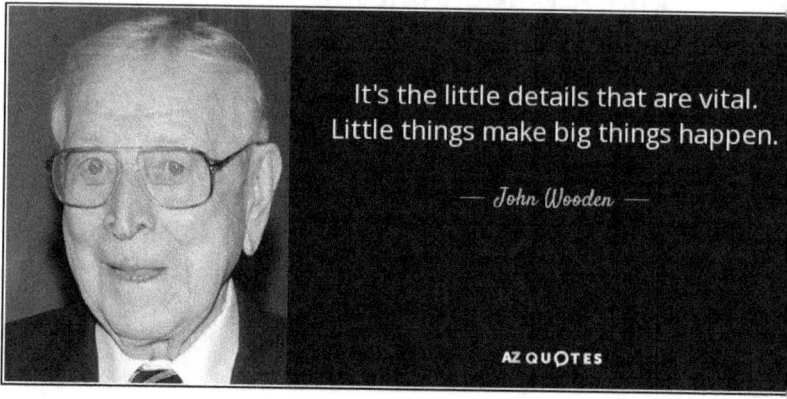

Professionalism is not thinking about the big things; professionalism is thinking about everything.

d. The Boss Values Productivity *and* People

Many motivational speakers and coaches, such as Tony Robbins, have focused more on the positive aspects of being a leader and the negative aspects of being a boss or pointing out the problems with bad bosses. They spread a negative perception of bosses and a positive perception of leaders. This is also why people follow leaders or try to be a leader instead of a boss.

The reality is too many leaders pay more attention to self-promotion rather than valuing the productivity and development of the organization.

Great bosses always focus on business goals, results, and success. Productivity must come first because the organization hires people to achieve the goal. The organizational goal is why people are employed, and great bosses focus more on achieving business success than keeping people happy.

This doesn't mean bosses don't value people. But they work best with effective and capable people who focus on reaching the organization's goal.

I had a bad hiring experience in 2016. My partners and I established a consulting firm and an institute. At the same time, I was also busy working as a Public Relations and Business Promotion Director of the Afghanistan Chamber of Commerce and Investment. My partners and I were also working with other organizations, so we hired a CEO to manage our business. He seemed to be an outstanding candidate with excellent relationship-building and communication skills and enough management knowledge. Unfortunately, he could not help us achieve our goals.

Among other factors, the main reason for his lack of success was that the CEO was trying to be a friend rather than a boss. Personal relationships were more important than the goals of the organization. For example, if an employee was late, they were advised not to repeat the problem. Still, no disciplinary warnings were given, and no actions were taken, so employees often ignored the advice because the Boss was too friendly.

Employees thought of the CEO as a friend and not a boss. So we replaced him with someone with more maturity and experience, someone who was straightforward and had clear expectations. Soon students and lecturers were on time. He recorded and asked about staff absences and focused on results, not on making people happy. His reward was the growth of the business.

Increase value and happiness through productivity, results, and building a strong team.

e. <u>The Boss Takes Command</u>

Jack Ma, the owner of Alibaba, says, "We have all kinds of animals. People talk, people don't talk, people work hard, and people never work; this is an amazing company ecosystem that makes the company very, very colorful."

I also have had the same experience. In my company, some people had energy and worked honestly, but others didn't. Some people were intelligent, and some were lazy. Thus, only smart bosses can lead such businesses.

Managing staff in multinational organizations and getting outstanding results can be challenging. Effective bosses have the confidence and the power to manage such companies. You will not be successful if you can't hire, fire, implement the protocol, and maintain control.

In one of my businesses, another CEO I hired was not maintaining control because employees were selling company secrets to competitors. He was not paying attention and this was a costly mistake. This experience was what taught me to be a boss and have full control, develop my own system, and have the courage to command, hire and fire.

Great bosses take command and manage the business. Institutions fail not because of their low-level employees but because bosses can't give direction or insist on changed behavior. It takes courage to establish control over what employees do and how they do it.

f. <u>The Boss Inspires by Being Clear</u>

Inspiration without clarity is useless. The Boss knows the goal is to create an atmosphere of outstanding results, punctuality, and self-discipline. The employee is paid to perform specific tasks and to know how to do the job; if they cannot do this, the organization loses.

Those who don't reach those goals may face warnings, decreased benefits or termination. The Boss must be straightforward, direct, and frank with employees. A great boss focuses on the employee's growth, recording the employee's activities, evaluating the staff, and managing the workplace.

The Boss's responsibility is to make the goals clear.

g. Leaders Say, "Let's Go!" but the Boss Says, "Go!"

This quote from George E M Kelly romanticizes leaders: "Remember the difference between a boss and a leader. A boss says, 'Go!' A leader says, 'Let's go!'" But we need good bosses to tell their people, "Go!" The Boss trusts his people. Some leaders solve problems with you but don't leave you alone. The Boss says, "Go!" and lets workers do their jobs.

Bosses are downgraded for letting employees work on their own. But the Boss is doing a great job. When a boss hires someone for a position, he trusts they can handle the pressure and get great results.

The Boss gives freedom to employees to work independently. This is the best way to support staff.

h. <u>The Boss Knows Profits Can Change the World</u>

Profits are essential in life and business. Some believe bosses put profits over people and are more interested in processes and proving themselves than in having happy and fulfilled employees. Although bosses focus on profits, it doesn't mean they don't consider the employees. The Boss pays a handsome salary, provides a great working environment, and facilitates the promotion process, benefiting employees.

Tony Robbins[9] says, "Leaders are ultimately driven not by profits and processes but by a powerful vision. They want to change the world, create something new and make a difference in people's lives. They're just as interested in the journey as

---

[9] Tony Robbins is an American author, coach, speaker, and philanthropist. He is known for his infomercials, seminars, and self-help books including the books Unlimited Power and more

they are in the destination. Leaders know when they put people first and allow or encourage them to live their purpose in life, profits will come naturally."

A boss believes profits and processes verify your vision and give you a clear picture. Most people have the vision but don't know how to achieve it. Bosses believe to achieve your vision, you need to know the profit, loss, and processes.

A boss believes more in starting small, changing themselves and their environment, being successful in their niche, and then positively impacting others' lives.

After successfully building the organization, the Boss can think about changing the world.

Be your Own Boss

i. **The Boss Has the Right Mindset**

The Boss focuses on growth and success, achieving a specific goal without wasting time. Leaders think about long-term vision and objectives, political issues, values, and building a team outside the business. We don't need leaders. Great bosses are needed to initiate and run successful businesses.

Followers come with leaders, but bosses don't want followers. They want doers, risk-takers, and out-of-the-box thinkers. While leaders are trying to figure out how to be more popular and visionary, bosses are growing the business. Be the Boss. That takes work.

Being a boss is not just a position; it's a mindset. Anyone can be a leader.

j. __The Boss Has a Clear Vision__

It is wrong that bosses don't have a vision. The Boss has a clear vision, mission, direction, strategic goal, and roadmap. They know where their final destination is and how to get there. That is why bosses are successful and can effectively lead their teams in a standard and unified direction to achieve the vision.

"Vision is the art of seeing what is invisible to others."

Jonathan Swift

k. <u>The Boss Is Self-Disciplined</u>

The Boss is self-disciplined. She loves protocols, being on time, using time effectively, working under pressure, and doing what she loves. She has self-discipline and understands what to do and when to do it.

If you're the Boss, nobody will ask you to get to work, stop watching movies or pick up the slack.

"Self-discipline is the drumbeat of success, the heartbeat of personal growth, and the counter beat of instant gratification. Follow the beat."

Julian Mather

I. <u>**The Boss Expects People to Succeed**</u>

The Boss doesn't pursue friendships at work. Instead, they focus on the goal and want their employees to do the same. Bosses evaluate the business, the employees, and the environment constantly. They love professional, qualified, and committed people and soon weed out everyone else.

I learned much from a very demanding boss by focusing and becoming results-oriented. Initially, he would be very frustrated with me because I was not meeting his expectations. I was tempted to resign, but then I realized I was not doing anything extraordinary, just the bare minimum. I was used to working with easygoing bosses and not paying attention to details.

So I challenged myself not to give my Boss any reason to be upset with me. I worked to become the best fit for the job, and I achieved my Boss's goals on time. He began to appreciate me and have a much more positive attitude toward me. I began to see positive changes in every area of my life. Soon he was educating and grooming me to be the best I could be. Eventually, we even became friends.

Many employees resigned because of the workload and a focused boss, which allowed the organization to find employees with the right qualifications, the ability to work under pressure, and the desire to pursue the organization's goals.

Great bosses help us succeed, be more focused, feel valued, and surround ourselves with like-minded people.

m. The Boss Has Strong People Skills

Bosses know how to handle workload pressures and resolve conflicts without upsetting people. The Boss also works to please and keep customers. He has internal and external responsibilities. Besides managing internal organizational issues, bosses also work on relationships as they find new customers, partners, and investors.

6. The Boss Avoids These Mistakes

a. <u>The Boss Isn't Disrespectful of Other Opinions</u>

Many startups fail because bosses fail to value their employees' thoughts and opinions. Running a business needs brainstorming and a well-organized team.

To be an effective boss and have a sustainable business, respect your subordinates' ideas and learn from them.

b. <u>The Boss Isn't Inconsistent with Decisions</u>

Once, I worked with a supervisor on a branding manual. She focused on the logo design and asked us to bring samples. We all designed and shared our samples, but she didn't like any of them.

Her expectations were not clear. I tried to read her mind regarding the design. Somehow I understood what she wanted, and I started working. I came up with my three best designs, explained the significance of the specific colors, fonts, and elements I chose, and drew the design flow.

Finally, she agreed and selected one of my designs with some minor changes. After I made the changes, she approved and signed off on the final logo. Soon she asked me to design other promotional materials and update the social media pages accordingly.

A few days later, someone else brought another design, and she accepted that design and ignored the approved one. My work took almost six months to be finalized. So don't be okay with one thing one day and then not okay with it the next. Sending mixed signals and an inconsistent message will eventually drive an employee into a despondent stupor. If they "can't win," no matter how much they try to do what you want, they'll soon give up trying.

Consistency and sound decisions support the organization and are a more economical use of time.

c. **Bosses Do Not Lose Control of Their Emotions**

Mark Twain[10] said: "Getting angry is easy. Anyone can do that. But getting angry in the right way in the right amount at the right time, now that is hard."

Before getting angry, put yourself in the other person's shoes and respond accordingly. Don't lose your self-control or temper. Stay calm and solve problems with a relaxed mind. Anger or a display of strong emotion is justified sometimes, but good bosses have control over their feelings. They aren't emotionally volatile. A volatile boss isn't the "rock" people need, but instead, a drifting buoy buffeted and beat around by the winds of adversity and other people's actions. Being intense is okay. Being

---

[10] Mark Twain, was an American writer, humorist, entrepreneur, publisher, and lecturer. He was lauded as the "greatest humorist the United States has produced", and William Faulkner called him "the father of American literature"

quick to be positive is good. But being easy to anger is not.[11]

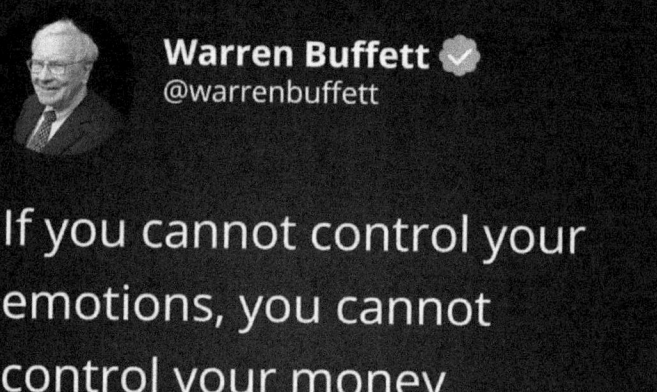

---

[11] Max Klein, Family Man. Leader. 3x Top Writer. MBA Strategy and Management. Marine Corps Veteran. Winemaker. emaxklein@icloud.com

d. <u>The Boss Doesn't Bother Employees on Vacation</u>

People need a break from work even if you're a good boss. They need family time. Family is more important than work for most people. Most people work to earn money and to care for their family's needs. So when you pester them with work when they are with family, it rubs people the wrong way. Occasionally, it's necessary, but always tell the employee you don't want to contact them but need them for a short time. They'll understand and be happy to help if it's not your standard MO (modus operandi)[12] to bother them. Max Klein said, "And never make them feel guilty for taking time off they've earned accordingly."

---

[12] A Latin phrase meaning "mode of operating. It refers to someone's habits of working, particularly in the context of business.

Let employees enjoy their time off. Bother them only if absolutely necessary.

e. The Boss Doesn't Tell Employees, "You Are Lucky to Have a Job."

Never tell your employees they are lucky they work there. It's the other way around. The Boss is fortunate to have honest, qualified, and professional employees.

f. <u>The Boss Isn't Mistrustful</u>

As a boss, you need to keep the organization's secrets, and you also need to share information with your subordinates. So before you hire a person, do as much research as possible, clear your doubts, have guarantee letters, ask questions, sign the contract, and mention the critical issues. Then when you hire them, value and trust them. The more you trust employees, the more they will see their future in your business. There are several ways a boss shows a lack of trust in their employees - micromanaging, refusing to give all the information needed, or not believing in your team. Employees can't thrive if they aren't given the room to do so.

The Boss also doesn't spy or interfere in personal Issues. Sometimes you may need to track and evaluate your employee's performance, but if you overdo it, it says you don't trust them. Don't do it.

It is terrible (and, in many places, illegal) to spy on or interfere with employees' personal issues. In some organizations, the Boss has security cameras at workstations that check everything. This is creepy and insulting. Only monetary and intelligence organizations can justify constant surveillance. The rest of your staff should feel at home. Max Klein states, "If you hired me to do a job, then let me do it. Spy on my results."

Treat your employees as if they were their own bosses. If they think the organization is their own, they will struggle and work even under pressure to achieve the organization's goals.

g. The Boss Doesn't Criticize Publicly and Praise Privately

Max Klein says the best leaders' general attitude is to take responsibility for failure and give credit for success. Never publicly criticize an employee. Never scold them in front of others because they will feel like they need to save face. The quickest way to be despised by someone is to criticize them publicly.

I had a boss who constantly denounced me publicly and praised me privately though I didn't know why. I learned later my Boss was criticizing me in public so others would be scared and obey him. So I stopped facing him publicly. Because of his behavior, I decided to start my own business and be my own Boss. Your employee is not your servant.

"Giving credit is like giving love — you get more of it by giving it away."
Unknown.

7. Thirteen Things a Boss Should Never Forget

a. <u>The Boss Pays Attention to Profit and Loss</u>

Bosses are responsible for the profit and loss of any deal they make. They understand how to lose money in the right way to generate high revenue. Bosses may ignore earnings initially, but that changes as their earnings do. When I started my own business, I did not expect revenue for the first six months based on my plan. Fortunately, I got a project within three months, which meant I had to keep track of my earnings.

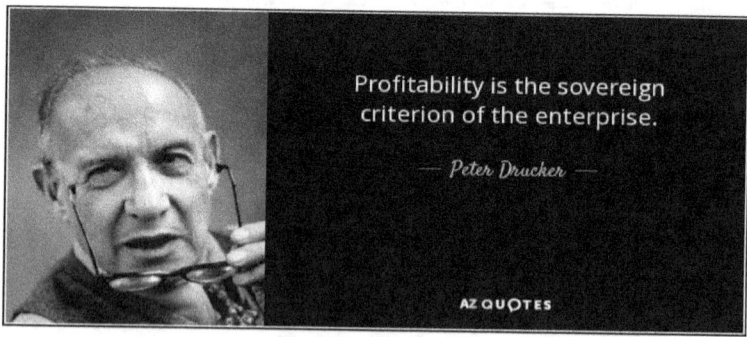

b. <u>The Boss Values Time</u>

Time management is the Boss's ability to split time between different projects or tasks for maximum productivity. Great bosses value their own time and know how to manage employees' time effectively.

c. <u>The Boss Is Straightforward</u>

Aimee Spencer explains that being straightforward is the bridge to authenticity and self-compassion. Even though it might hurt people sometimes, you are not trying to be rude. You are just being honest. Bosses believe being straightforward allows you to be realistic. It bolsters your courage and frees you to be who you are. Sometimes direct bosses are viewed as impolite or impatient, but direct communication is an excellent habit!

d. The Boss Knows When to Say "No."

Bosses understand the importance of focus, dedication, and time; that is why they have the power to say "no" to many other things. William Leith[13] says, "We live in a world where "yes" is the default. Unfortunately, "No" carries an unseen force that can make it feel exaggeratedly oppressive, almost a dirty word.

We're told saying "No" is a negative thing that hurts those around us and can cause us to miss out on new opportunities. No wonder so many people are uncomfortable using this word. Our failure to say "No" stems from wanting to make others feel comfortable. This notion needs to be shaken off immediately. Being unable to say "No" is not only unfair to ourselves but the other person as well."

---

[13] William Leith is the author of The Hungry Years: Confessions of a Food Addict. June 2020, my problem with money and many more.

When you say, "No," you're eliminating unnecessary excess.

e. <u>**The Boss Keeps Notes and Records**</u>

As a boss, you need to take notes. This will help you organize what you hear in meetings. If someone claims Topic X wasn't covered or you forget the essential meeting minutes, you can refer to your notes.[14] Bosses use pen and notebook all the time, taking notes of the minutes of meetings, emails, negotiations, presentations, staff evaluations, customer suggestions, and objections about critical issues. These notes help them make outstanding decisions in the future. So don't forget to keep the bullet points and valuable information.

> **"I take notes like some people take drugs." Tim Ferris**

---

[14] Lighthouse block: <u>Why Managers Should Take Notes</u> (getlighthouse.com)

d. The Boss Trusts in First Impressions

Many bosses know who they are dealing with at the first hello. They also often have an accurate impression of the staff, customers, and partners.

Bosses know that the first impression is the last impression.

f. **The Boss Follows the Protocol**

Bosses say "No" to the organization's personal friendships and family relationships. They follow the protocol and discipline within the organization.

Once I remembered a vacancy available in the organization I worked for when my Boss's brother was looking for a job. I asked him if he could hire his brother. My Boss said, "Yes, I have the power to hire him, but I don't want him to be a part of this organization. If I hire him, I am not following the rules of the organization for everybody. If I make any exceptions, it will have a negative impact on the organization's discipline." It was incredible how committed he was to the organization's discipline and professionalism.

Be your Own Boss

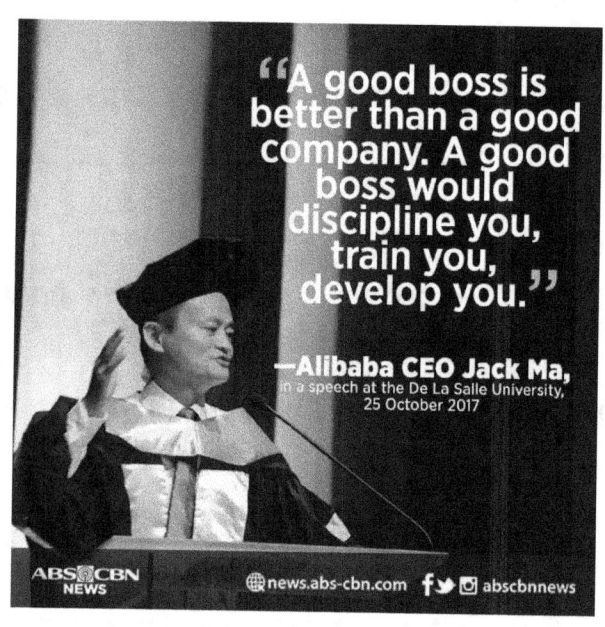

g. **The Boss Has Action Plans**

The Boss never forgets the action plans - hourly, daily, weekly, monthly, quarterly, and annually. They write and follow them by conducting regular meetings and workshops. A successful boss doesn't forget this.

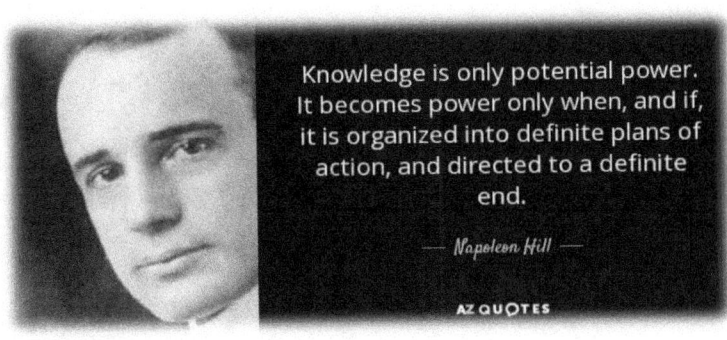

I learned much from my Boss while working as a communications expert with Mediothek. At 9:00 a.m., he would ask us to share our daily plans and reports at the end of the day. We would have weekly meetings and make action plans for the week. We were expected to share our daily action plans and reports to finalize what we had promised in our weekly meetings.

Our organization was successful because we used our resources effectively and efficiently.

Bosses are people of actions and results.

h. <u>The Boss Builds an Outstanding Team</u>

We can learn team building and cooperation from musicians. The singer is usually the face of the group, like the Boss. The musicians behind the singer are the team who supports the singer (Boss). When everyone performs professionally and enjoys their roles, the song and music touch hearts. We unintentionally say, "Wow!" Great bosses always work to build an outstanding team.

Teamwork makes the dream work.

or

"No one can whistle a symphony. It takes a whole orchestra to play it."

H.E. Luccock

i. <u>The Boss is Results- or Outcomes-Oriented</u>

Bosses are results-oriented people; they don't love excuses or reasons. They love the team that provides outstanding results. Results are like a drug for the Boss, who is like an addict without a fix until they get results. I once had a boss who was miserable until the work was done perfectly and he got results. He would hardly eat or drink. All he could do was work, think, and focus on finding creative ways to solve problems. I don't recommend this approach, but he always got the best results.

The best medicine for a boss's pain is on-time and exceptional results.

When I resigned from my position, my Boss asked for a short meeting; he was impressive and challenging. He asked why I was leaving. I answered honestly that I had been offered a position in another organization. He congratulated me and said, "I am sad about your leaving but happy about your promotion and advancement."

Then he said something important. "Did you know," he asked, "I had many complaints and a lot of gossip about you during your time with me, and I didn't act on it or even mention it to you? I didn't decide against you because you were results-oriented and had an outstanding record with me."

Workers can complain and gossip when they are under pressure or feeling controlled. My Boss taught me how bosses look at results instead.

I am writing this book because I have worked with different bosses and then became a boss myself. I have been successful because I learned from good and bad bosses and led my team carefully.

8. What Kills Your Career as a Boss

a. <u>Not Making Your Business a Full-Time Commitment.</u>

If you quit your job to be your own Boss, you may suddenly have more time on your hands. In many ways, this can be wonderful. You might be able to take your children to school and pick them up at the end of the school day. You might be able to get some household chores done, some that have been waiting for a long time. Using this newfound freedom to relax and meet friends is also tempting. Don't fall into this trap. Remember this: You are working for free until you have generated customers and revenue. This may take a while, and the soonest way to get to that point is to begin working immediately and put in as much time as possible. Being an entrepreneur is a full-time job whether you get paid or not.

Yes, you can have more time with your kids or at home, but your main priority is your business when you work.

"Commitment is an act, not a word." Jean-Paul Sartre

Be your Own Boss

b. **Not Having a Written Schedule**

This goes hand-in-hand with the first warning. You must have a *written* schedule for the day and the week. How will you fill each hour? What will you do during those hours? Because you are free to create your own schedule, you can plan in a way that works best for you and even your family, but plan on putting in a lot of hours towards your business. Brian Tracy says we work forty hours just for survival. How many hours a week over forty will you work?

There are different methods to track your schedule, e.g., using a planner, Google Calendar, and many other online tools and applications. I suggest using the e-calendar because the software will notify you of your upcoming commitments.

"Goals that are not written down are just wishes." Annie Dillard

c. <u>Not Having Clear and Written Goals</u>

You must have written goals, not only for your business overall but on a day-to-day basis. You can write your goals in your planner. Caution: Don't forget to review your goals regularly, even several times a day, until you have completed your daily goals. Then make new goals.

> **"Only three percent of adults have written goals, and everyone else works for them."**
>
> Brian Tracy

d. Not Having a Reason Why

Why are you in business? The first and most obvious answer is to make money, but is that the only reason? As mentioned, what problem or problems do you want to solve - for yourself, your family, society, or even the world? Frederich Nietzsche said, "He who has a why to live for can bear almost any how." The same is true for your business. Why did you decide to be your own Boss? What do you want from life?

"The two most important days in life are the day you born and the day you discover the reason why."

Mark Twain

e. <u>Not Talking to the Most Important People.</u>

Being your own Boss can be a challenging and even scary experience for you and those around you. Do you have the approval and support of those closest to you? If you are married, is your spouse completely behind your idea? Do those closest to you think you can be your own Boss? We may not always get the answers we want, but sometimes that is the best way to learn before making a mistake.

"Give importance to those people who give importance to you."

Luffina Lourduraj

f. <u>Not Having Guidance.</u>

Getting guidance through books, the internet, courses, mentors, other entrepreneurs, or support groups is essential. Just because you chose to be your own Boss doesn't mean you should do it alone. There are always new things to learn, and what you know can save time and money.

> **"Be a student. Stay open and willing to learn from everyone and anyone. Being a student means you have room for new input."**
>
> Wayne Dyer

g. <u>Not Taking Care of Yourself.</u>

As important as it is to work, it is just as important to take care of yourself. Proper sleep and nutrition are vital. You're undertaking something wholly new, and it can take a lot out of you, so make sure you put it back into yourself.

"Almost everything will work again if you unplug it for a few minutes, including you."

Anne Lamott

9. How to Behave like a Boss until You Are a Boss

Being your own Boss takes time and planning. Begin developing the Boss Mindset now! You may not be ready to start immediately, but here are some behaviors you can practice until you can start running your own business.

a. Take Complete Responsibility for Your Job.

Make sure you do your job to the best of your ability, no matter what it is. You may be the newest employee or on the lowest rung of the ladder, but be the Boss of your job and be responsible for completing every task quickly and well. Whatever you are, be the best at it. Be your own Boss even if you aren't the Boss yet.

"We must all suffer one of two things: the pain of discipline or the pain of regret or disappointment."

Jim Rohn

b. <u>Learn Every Aspect of Your Job.</u>

No matter what you do, there are always things to learn. You will improve and be more passionate about your work as you learn. In addition, you will want to learn more, which will cause you to improve even more. Knowledge is not power, but applied knowledge is. This means reading and learning more as often as you can.

"Details make perfection, and perfection is not a detail."
Leonardo Da Vinci

c. <u>Take on Extra Responsibilities.</u>

When possible, and if it won't interfere with doing your job well, ask your supervisor if you can take on extra responsibilities. When given an extra assignment, complete it as quickly and as well as possible. Then ask for another. Repeat.

> "Unless you try to do something beyond what you have already mastered, you will never grow."
>
> Ralph Waldo Emerson

d. <u>Practice Your People Skills.</u>

We are only as good as our relationships. None of us can do it alone. Most of all, you never know who can help (or harm) you, so do your best to work well with everyone. You may not like everyone, but the people you find difficult are actually the best vehicles to practice your people skills.

"Manage your relationships. Great relationships may not be profitable, but bad ones always result in losses."

Tarun Sharma

e. <u>**Work Longer Hours.**</u>

If you can do it, arrive early and stay late. An extra hour early or an hour later every day adds up to five extra hours a week. If you work 50 weeks a year, that's 250 extra hours a year. How good would you be at your job if you put in that much time?

"You can't be afraid of hard work or long hours. Sacrifice is important." Jerry Bruckheimer

f. **Develop Yourself.**

Read, exercise, take care of your body, and get sleep. Develop yourself on every level. If you feel better, you will do better.

"There is only one corner of the universe you can be certain of improving, and that's your own self." Aldous Huxley

10. Conclusion

This book is the shortcut to being your own Boss and driving your life the way you want. Although this is the end of the book, it's the beginning of your journey. Refer to this book often for reminders and encouragement. Being your own Boss takes courage, discipline, people skills, and hard work, but when you taste success and realize you enjoy work and life more, it is all worth it.

As a boss, you should build a team where everybody finds themselves as a boss. The reason I had a successful business was my strong team. In my team, everyone is a boss. So start your business, be your own Boss and build a strong team where everyone considers themselves a boss.

Being Your Own Boss is one of the most enjoyable and challenging decisions to make.

There's no time like the present to take the leap, enjoy the benefits, and prepare yourself for tough times. Create an idea based on your vision, establish your goals, and start your business energetically. You'll be glad you did.

To start your business, read my next book, <u>Start Your Own Business Now</u>.

11. References

1. Wickman, G. and Boer, R., 2016. *How to be a Great Boss*. BenBella Books, Inc..

2. Dealy, D.M., Dealy, M.D. and Thomas, A.R., 2004. *Defining the really great Boss*. Greenwood Publishing Group.

3. Lazear, E.P., Shaw, K.L. and Stanton, C.T., 2015. The value of bosses. *Journal of Labor Economics*, 33(4), pp.823-861.

4. Shaw, K.L., 2019. Bosses matter: The effects of managers on workers' performance. *IZA World of Labor*.

5. Eikenberry, K. and Harris, G., 2011. *From Bud to Boss: Secrets to a successful transition to remarkable leadership*. John Wiley & Sons.

6. Boutillier, S. and Uzunidis, D., 2020. Entrepreneur: Etymological Bases. In Encyclopedia of Creativity, Invention,

Innovation and Entrepreneurship (pp. 803-806). Cham: Springer International Publishing.

Online Resources:

1. Nicoline van der Sijs, (October 27, 2010) 'Baas' is biggest Dutch language export. https://www.dutchnews.nl/news/2010/10/baas_is_biggest_dutch_language/

2. Surbhi S, (August 5, 2017). Difference Between Boss and Leader. https://keydifferences.com/difference-between-boss-and-leader.html

3. St Bonaventure University Online (May 11, 2020) Leader Versus Boss: What's the Difference? https://online.sbu.edu/news/leader-versus-boss#:~:text=The%20terms%20boss%20and%20leader,and%20leader%20have%20different%20connotations.

4. Entrepreneurship, Series on Entrepreneurial Culture, (May 8, 2009) Etymology of the Word Entrepreneur, https://www.davelerner.com/latest-posts/david_b_lerner/2009/05/etymology-of-the-word-entrepreneur.html

5. Surbhi S, (July 26, 2018), Difference Between Businessman and Entrepreneur. https://keydifferences.com/difference-between-businessman-and-entrepreneur.html

6. Tabitha Njogu, (02/21/2022) Difference Between Entrepreneur and Businessman, http://www.differencebetween.net/business/difference-between-entrepreneur-and-businessman/

7. Michael Keating, (July 30, 2014) Difference Between A Boss And A Leader Explained. Learn The Details Of Why A Boss Is Different Than A Leader (octatools.com)

8. Elena Hudgens, (August 23, 2021) Entrepreneur vs Investor: Which One Are You? https://thehustlestory.com/entrepreneur-vs-investor-which-one-are-

you/#:~:text=While%20being%20optimistic%2C%20an%20entrepreneur,the%20quantitatve%20and%20financial%20side.

9. Julian Mather, (Sep 19, 2017) Self Discipline: The Missing Piece of the Employee Engagement Puzzle. https://medium.com/@julianmather/self-discipline-the-missing-piece-of-the-employee-engagement-puzzle-973f5a29fab8

10. Max Klein, (Mar 22, 2021) 10 Things a Boss Should Never Do, https://emaxklein.medium.com/10-things-a-boss-should-never-do-7415a224a2ea

11. David Shedd (Oct 18, 2016) The 7 Don'ts of Employee Motivation. https://www.linkedin.com/pulse/7-donts-employee-motivation-david-shedd

12. Devra Gartenstein, (Oct 19, 2018), Social Responsibility of a Sole Proprietorship. https://yourbusiness.azcentral.com/social-responsibility-sole-proprietorship-13178.html

13. Desiree Peralta, (Dec 16, 2020) You Will Never Be Rich If You Keep Doing These 10 things.
https://themakingofamillionaire.com/you-will-never-be-rich-if-you-keep-doing-these-10-things-8c9677bc06b0

14. Dorothy Neufeld (March 29, 2022) The Richest People in the World in 2022.
https://www.visualcapitalist.com/richest-people-in-the-world-2022/

15. Mike Kaeding, (Jul 1, 2018) Treat Employees Well and the Rest Will Take Care of Itself.
https://www.linkedin.com/pulse/treat-employees-well-rest-take-care-itself-mike-kaeding

16. Atul Malikram (Jul 25, 2022) No - it's a small word that packs a lot of power.
https://www.linkedin.com/pulse/its-small-word-packs-lot-power-atul-malikram-1c?trk=article-ssr-frontend-pulse_more-articles_related-content-card

17. Ben Schwencke, (29 Apr 2022) Why Attention to Detail is Important in the Workplace.
https://www.testpartnership.com/blog/why-attention-to-detail-important.html

18. Martin, M. (2020, July 7). Logo Design and First Impressions. Spade Design.
https://www.kompasiana.com/image/cindyfernanda3031/612cae8f31a2877f3d0bf182/101-cara-membuat-first-impression-yang-baik-di-mata-orang?page=1

19. Brigette Hyacinth (May 24, 2022) A Bad Job With a Good Boss Is Better Than a Good Job With a Bad Boss.
https://thriveglobal.com/stories/a-bad-job-with-a-good-boss-is-better-than-a-good-job-with-a-bad-boss/

20. Melina Miller, (March 13, 2020) Is Marketing Research Important for Small Business Owners?
https://www.melinakmiller.com/is-marketing-research-important-for-small-bus/

21. Tony Robbins, HOW TO BE YOUR OWN BOSS, https://www.tonyrobbins.com/business/how-to-be-your-own-boss/#:~:text=To%20discover%20how%20to%20become,top%20skills%20and%20your%20experience.

22. Skye Schooley (Jun 29, 2022) How to Find Your Business Niche. https://www.businessnewsdaily.com/6748-business-niche-characteristics.html

www.ingramcontent.com/pod-product-compliance
Lightning Source LLC
Chambersburg PA
CBHW070235220526
45465CB00004B/1424